A Word from the Publisher – Pegasus Books

In the cynical, fast-paced world we live in, it is rare to find a voice in a writer so focused on inspiring us, and more importantly, our children. Sommer Rose's *Inspiring Quotes for the Youth* is a refreshing break from the typical commercial-driven (and sometimes unprincipled) titles published for kids today. Rather, it offers spiritual reflections and insights that the entire family can discuss and revisit over time.

The author has included a provocative discussion aid at the back of the book to help stimulate moving conversations and honest communication between parents and children, between teachers and students and between inspired youth.

As the publisher of *Inspiring Quotes for the Youth*, I am dedicated to work to bring this book into thousands of households and schools, where the character of our children take form, for good or bad. Beyond that, I will make myself and the book available custom printing, distinctive for groups or school districts and for special events

In addition, Sommer Rose, the book's author will make herself available for speaking engagements, book club discussions and comment exchanges as she continues in this book series. We both look forward to working with you soon!

Thank you for your interest in this book and thank you for all you do to support our youth!

Sincerely,

Marcus McGee
Publisher, Pegasus Books
Media, ContentConnect

I0086675

Inspiring Quotes for the Youth

Sommer Rose

PEGASUS BOOKS

Pegasus Books
8165 Valley Green Drive
Sacramento, CA, 95823
www.pegasusbooks.net

First Edition: May 2017

Published in North America by Pegasus Books. For information, please contact Pegasus Books c/o Marcus McGee, 8165 Valley Green Drive, Sacramento, CA, 95823.

This book is a work of non-fiction. Although the author and publisher have made every effort to ensure that the information in this book was correct at press time, the author and publisher do not assume and hereby disclaim any liability to any party for any loss, damage, or disruption caused by errors or omissions, whether such errors or omissions result from negligence, accident, or any other cause.

Library of Congress Cataloguing-In-Publication Data
Sommer Rose
Inspiring Quotes for the Youth/Sommer Rose— 2nd ed
p. cm.
Library of Congress Control Number: 2017906977
ISBN – 978-1-941859-66-7
1. BIOGRAPHY & AUTOBIOGRAPHY / General. 2. YOUNG ADULT NONFICTION / General. 3. YOUNG ADULT NONFICTION / Inspirational & Personal Growth. 4. BODY, MIND & SPIRIT / Inspiration & Personal Growth. 5. FAMILY & RELATIONSHIPS / General.

10 9 8 7 6 5 4 3 2

Comments about *Inspiring Quotes for the Youth* and requests for additional copies, book club rates and author speaking appearances may be addressed to Sommer Rose or Pegasus Books c/o Marcus McGee, 8165 Valley Green Drive, Sacramento, CA, 95823, or you can send your comments and requests via e-mail to mmcgee@pegasusbooks.net.

Also available as an eBook from Internet retailers and from Pegasus Books

Printed in the United States of America

This book is dedicated to my daughters Kayla & Camille

Authors' Note

My experiences raising my own children and being around teenagers and young adults sparked my interest to do more, get more involved with the community and reveal my visions. As adults, we have a duty to better ourselves and be good examples.

We know right from wrong, so we should lead in the right way. In doing better, the message for positive growth must be heard. Encouragement for good decision-making must be spoken.

We are all on a life journeys. No matter how we get through the obstacles we are facing with along the way, our results are a direct product of our decisions and actions. Whatever we do cannot be "taken back" or "done over." We should give situations a good amount of thought before making final decisions, which I hope are intelligent decisions.

This book introduces quotes that initiate good decision-making on a daily basis. They are quotes I've created to guide our youth in positive directions and keep them on the paths of growth and success. Their future is golden.

It's important that young people value the life they live by building their self-esteem and having an understanding of the power they hold. I've written seventy quotes, which recommend positive thinking as well as productive planning and setting future goals.

My focus is to promote healthy living including thinking intelligently and making sure those thoughts are followed by smart actions.

Introduction

As we grow and experience more things in life, we can witness change. We see kids grow into young adults. We see different mentalities and recognize different directions this society has taken. It becomes more definite that we are becoming numb to immoral behaviors.

We observe actions that show there is a thin line between good and evil. I am a person who sees the world as a diverse place, a place where it is still difficult to accept differences. The true nature of our existence is to co-exist. Life is about change and being different.

Many times, when I go out in public, I see bad influences. Families need more stability. A better foundation must be set for our children. My background involved consistency from my mother and my father. They were committed to being present in my and my brother's life. They instilled morals and religion as the fundamental guidance to raising us. With my mother's strong dedication and hands-on relationship, she taught us entrepreneur skills that opened the doors towards our futures.

I challenge every adult to speak up when you notice out-of-line behavior from the youth (cursing, being rude or disrespectful, sagging pants). Maybe their parents aren't present in their lives to correct them. They may have unfortunate backgrounds where they need help. If we can help with encouraging words, then we should.

Inspiring Quotes
for the Youth

hello ADVENTURE Laugh BE WHO
you are

Once UPON ENJOY hope
A TIME Love

BE BRAVE, BE HAPPY

SMILE

BE Joyful NOW

happy

TODAY IS YOUR DAY

BRAVERY
IS BELIEVING
in
yourself

you are
MY
Sunshine

DREAM

Joyful

There are good things inside you

There is no one else like you in the world. That's what makes you a unique individual. A person may look like you or sound like you, but you are your own special person.

Love everything about you. If you don't, who will? It all starts with caring, respecting and believing in yourself. When you believe in yourself, your future is promising. You will dream big and wish for amazing things to happen.

When those dreams and thoughts come, talk about them to your parents, family members and friends. It validates your interest and goals.

Love yourself before you look for love from anyone else.

You are unique, express your creativity.

Talk about your dreams. You will speak them into existence.

Weigh all of your options before committing to anything.

It's not always good to make quick decisions. When challenging situations arise, take your time before deciding what to do. You always have other choices, but if you act too fast, you cut out a possible better option.

Never quit; always finish what you start.

Be a leader. Leaders make a difference.

Be honest, honesty builds trust.

Speak the truth, a lie will get you in more trouble.

Learn to be silent. Silence brings peace. Too much talking brings problems.

Think before you speak. Make sure what you say is what you really mean.

People have a hard time telling the truth because they fear the consequences. But there's actually more work involved in lying. A story has to be made-up to convince a person you're telling the truth.

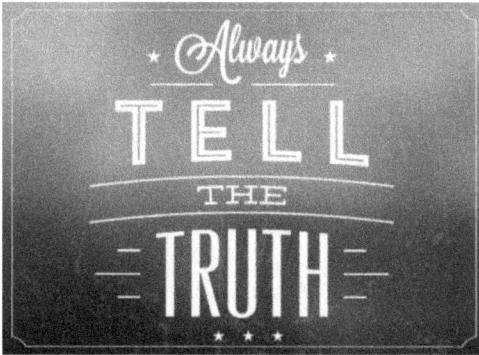

There have been many times when I wish I hadn't said something that I said. Times when I wanted to take what I said back, because after saying it, then thinking about it, I was in fact wrong. I've learned not to say everything that comes to mind.

I also learned that a person's tone and approach to a situation must be appropriate and not over reacted. Explaining the truth builds trust. When lies start they keep going.

A person has to remember the lie they told which builds into more lies and causes ongoing confusion, inconsistencies and distrust.

A bad attitude is unattractive.

It's important to control your emotions. Don't be too emotional.

Avoid cursing. Using bad words shows a lack of intelligence.

I cringe when I hear bad language. It's very disrespectful and does not sound or look good. Expressing how you feel, using words with meaning, shows intelligence and self-control.

You can learn something every day if you listen.

Express love. It generates peace and unity.

Conflicts will come; approach them calmly.

Unfortunately, bad things will happen in our lives. It's important that we try to remain positive when dealing with difficult situations. Having a humble and patient attitude makes it easier for us to get through hard times.

Education lasts a lifetime. Friends come and go.

Worry about your own life. You only have to live it.

In other words, mind your own business. Don't get involved in everyone else's. Don't be nosey.

Popularity is not important. Focus on education before focusing on friends.

Who cares what anyone thinks? They don't matter.

Friends can be cool, but they can also be cruel. Keep your friends at a distance. They are nice to have at times. Make sure they have good intensions when it comes to your friendship.

If a friend turns out to be a distraction, move on. Friends will come and friends will go.

It's important to stress that popularity is not important. Knowledge is important in life, which means focusing on school and going as far as possible in education.

Dealing with this problem of bullying, don't allow others to lower your self-esteem or your confidence. Speak up. Don't let a person make you feel like they have power over you.

Do not feed into gossip. Dismiss yourself from immature conversations.

Avoid wasting energy on things you can't control.

Don't be afraid to stand up for what you know is right.

Appreciate the wisdom of your elders. Respect the advice they give.

Recognize your strengths, build on them. Identify your weaknesses and eliminate them.

It doesn't matter what anyone says to do, the ultimate decision is on you.

Do not be lazy. Laziness can become a habit and will hold you back.

Time will not wait for you. Use the time you have wisely.

Do not sleep excessively. You will miss out on opportunities.

Be on time. It shows you are reliable.

When a person wastes time, it is lost forever, a missed opportunity for learning and growing. Every day lived should have purpose.

Stay focused on fulfilling a productive plan, such as furthering education or getting a job.

Kids spend too much time on the phone and Internet. With so many social media sites, it's all a distraction and can be negative.

Parents should monitor their child's phone usage and create a child-lock to block sites that are inappropriate.

Save your money. Money goes fast but comes slow.

Secure your own income. Be frugal. Don't depend on others

Limit unnecessary spending.

◇◇◇◇◇◇◇◇◇◇◇◇◇◇◇◇◇◇◇◇◇◇◇◇◇◇◇◇

It takes sacrifice in order to succeed.

Your parents want the best for you. Do what they say.

Be thankful for God's blessings. He blesses us every day.

Achieving success does not come easy. You may have to eliminate regular recreational activities to make time to handle business required to accomplish your goals.

◇◇◇◇◇◇◇◇◇◇◇◇◇◇◇◇◇◇◇◇◇◇◇◇◇◇◇◇

Do not avoid your problems. Find a solution for them.

Be polite; manners show great character.

Do not be jealous of another person's material. Work hard to get the things that you want.

The harder you work at your goals, the closer you will get to achieving them.

Do not doubt your ability to overcome challenges.

You can accomplish whatever you put your mind and energy into.

Make good choices. Choose to do the right thing. Good choices take you far.

I have experienced that dreams become a reality in my life and witnessed them happening in others. We have control over our future. It's up to us to make the most of the time we are given. Set high standards and challenge yourself to follow them.

It is one thing to set goals, but what actually counts are the steps taken to make those goals happen.

◇◇◇◇◇◇◇◇◇◇◇◇◇◇◇◇◇◇◇◇◇◇◇◇

Compliment more. There are good
qualities in everyone.

Give respect and expect it in return.

Admit when you are wrong.

◇◇◇◇◇◇◇◇◇◇◇◇◇◇◇◇◇◇◇◇◇◇◇◇

Laugh often. Expressing humor is healthy.

Be willing to help others when needed.

Pick your battles. Don't start an unnecessary argument.

~~~~~~~~~~~~~~~~~~~~~~~~~~~~~~~~~

Appreciate the simple things in life.

Keep a good attitude. Positive energy brings a happy productive day.

Commit to growth.

~~~~~~~~~~~~~~~~~~~~~~~~~~~~~~~~~

Believe in yourself.

I am smart. I am strong. I am beautiful.
I am brave.

Respect yourself. Your mind, body, and
soul.

◇◇◇◇◇◇◇◇◇◇◇◇◇◇◇◇◇◇◇◇◇◇◇◇◇◇◇◇

Try a new skill. You may be good at it!

Practice your skills often. You will get better.

Have confidence in yourself.

◇◇◇◇◇◇◇◇◇◇◇◇◇◇◇◇◇◇◇◇◇◇◇◇◇◇◇◇

Elevation is life. It is part of growth. It's important to enhance our strength to grow, our mind for higher intelligence and our spirit to keep a healthy soul.

There is always something new to learn. Find time to try a new skill.

Motivate yourself to experience something challenging and fun. It may turn out to be something you enjoy doing!

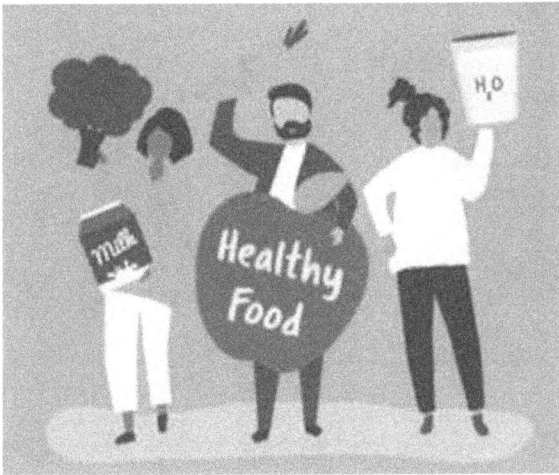

Cleanliness is Godliness. Clean as you go.

Maintain an organized life. Organization brings balance and order.

Eat healthy. You are what you eat. Moderation is the key.

Demand change for the better. Don't let an unrighteous soul linger.

Forgive and let go. Do not hold grudges.

Look forward to good things happening. Good thoughts bring good actions.

Change can be good, as long as it is to better ourselves. Changing a bad behavior is good. Choosing better friends is good for keeping positive energy in your circle. Surround yourself with people who are happy and optimistic!

◇✕◇✕◇✕◇✕◇✕◇✕◇✕◇✕◇✕◇✕◇✕◇✕◇✕◇

Forget the past but remember the importance of it.

Do not dwell on situations that have happened in the past. They will weigh on you and cause distraction. Instead, learning from the outcomes and understanding them can bring growth in the midst of hardship.

Don't do something you will regret later.

◇✕◇✕◇✕◇✕◇✕◇✕◇✕◇✕◇✕◇✕◇✕◇✕◇✕◇

Every new day brings new beginnings.
Fulfill what is good.

Be patient, good things come to those
who wait.

Create

Focus on stability.

Build a solid foundation that promotes future longevity.

Start building knowledge now. You can never learn to much, and it's never too late to learn.

Research all your interests. Time is limited. Narrow down to the top two or three careers and study their pathways to success!

My Favorite Quotes

1. *"Live as if you were to die tomorrow. Learn as if you were to live forever."*

–Mahatma Gandhi

Dream

2. *"A dream doesn't become reality through magic. It takes sweat, determination, and hard work."*

–Colin Powell

3. *"Education is the most powerful weapon that you can use to change the world."*

–Nelson Mandela

4. *It is easier to build strong children than to repair broken adults.*

—Fredrick Douglas

ABOUT THE AUTHOR

I'm a person who enjoys the creative aspects of life. As much as life is a challenge, it is also a treasure. I have worked at Kaiser Permanente in Sacramento, California as a Nutrition Partner for 14 years. I meet so many different individuals from many backgrounds and have learned so much since I've been there.

I enjoy mothering my two daughters who are 11 and 8. Together we enjoy gardening, riding bikes, skating, going to the movies, visiting relatives, playing games, etc. We enjoy listening to music as well.

As a child I played the trumpet and was a member of the jazz band. I learned the piano for a few years then spent most of my time playing tennis and basketball. I earned a tennis scholarship to Alabama A&M University where I studied journalism. I'm currently teaching myself the acoustic guitar.

I began enjoying writing in the fourth grade. I noticed myself extending spelling sentences into paragraphs and I'd always go over the assigned writing limit.

My teachers told me they looked forward to reading the writing assignments I turned in because they were always lengthy and interesting.

Teachers and others encouraged me to continue writing as much as possible, which lead to stories and short books. I entered my work in many book contests and received first and second place awards in most of them.

As I continued writing, it has become clear that writing will be a significant part of my future!

visit my website at www.sommerrose.net.

Exercises for Young Readers and Parents/Guardians

While reading my book, you'll find I have a specific focus that introduces many topics our youth face today. In order to narrow focus, my recommendation for this book is reading one page at a time, either by yourself, as a group or with a parent or guardian. After you have finished a page, please take the time to discuss each page as it relates to the following **five areas of life where everyone needs inspiration**:

#1. **Self-esteem.** What is it? Ask yourself: *Do I love myself? Do I have pride in myself? Do I believe in or care about my future? Do I set goals for myself?*

#2. **Making good decisions.** What is it? Ask yourself: *How do I know if I'm making a good decision?* If it is something good or positive and the outcome is good as well, it is most likely a good decision. Weigh your options before making a final decision. Know the consequences. If it is difficult to come to a conclusion, get advice from someone you trust.

#3. **Positive thinking.** What is it? Ask yourself: *Am I happy? Am I optimistic? Do I look forward to the future? Going to school? Playing sports? Am I being pressured into doing things I don't agree with or bullied at school?*

#4. **Showing respect.** What is it? Ask yourself: Do I respect myself and others? Do I speak with confidence and display good morals? Do I curse or listen to vulgar music? Do I like tattoos?

#5. **Furthering education.** What is it? Ask yourself: *Are there any classes or schoolwork I need extra help with? Have I or am I making plans to go to college? What are my career goals?*

Example: Begin at page one of this book. Read the page aloud together. Turn back to this page to discuss how each of the five areas above relate to the page you just read. Repeat this process as you continue the book to completion. Great job and good luck!